W9-ABU-029

Materials

Rock

Cassie Mayer

Heinemann Library
Chicago, Illinois

© 2008 Heinemann Library
a division of Reed Elsevier Inc.
Chicago, Illinois

Customer Service 888-454-2279
Visit our website at www.heinemannraintree.com

Picture research: Tracy Cummins and Heather Mauldin
Designed by Joanna Hinton-Malivoire
Printed in China by South China Printing Company Limited

12 11 10 09 08
10 9 8 7 6 5 4 3 2 1

ISBN-13: 978-1-4329-1622-0 (hc)
ISBN-13: 978-1-4329-1631-2 (pb)

The Library of Congress has cataloged the first edition as follows:
Mayer, Cassie.
  Rock / Cassie Mayer.
    p. cm. -- (Materials)
  Includes bibliographical references and index.
  ISBN 978-1-4329-1622-0 (hc) -- ISBN 978-1-4329-1631-2 (pb) 1. Rocks--Juvenile literature. 2. Petrology--Juvenile literature. I. Title.
  QE432.2.M29 2008
  552--dc22
                              2008005582

Acknowledgments
The author and publisher are grateful to the following for permission to reproduce copyright material: ©Corbis pp. **13** (Gaetano), **17** (Photo Images/Lee Snider); ©Getty Images pp. **8** (Lester Lefkowitz), **10** (Kevin Schafer); ©Heinemann Raintree pp. **6**, **9**, **20**, **22B**, **22T** (David Rigg); ©istockphoto p. **22M** (Mark Evans); ©Shutterstock pp. **4** (Martin Maun), **5** (Kristy Batie), **7** (Peter Kunasz), **11** (Vova Pomortzeff), **12** (Galyna Andrushko), **14** (Jane McIlroy), **15** (Jos Stover), **16** (Igor Smichkov), **18** (George Burba), **19** (Johanna Goodyear), **21** (Lucian Coman), **23B** (Martin Maun), **23M** (Igor Smichkov), **23T** (Jane McIlroy).

Cover image used with permission of ©Getty Images (D. Steele/Photo Access). Back cover image used with permission of ©Heinemann Raintree (David Rigg).

Every effort has been made to contact copyright holders of any material reproduced in this book. Any omissions will be rectified in subsequent printings if notice is given to the publisher.

Contents

What Are Rocks?

Rocks are in nature.

Rocks are many colors.

Rocks are many sizes.

Rocks are many shapes.

Rocks are hard.

Rocks are soft.

Rocks are big.

Rocks are small.

Where Are Rocks Found?

Rocks are above the ground.

Rocks are below the ground.

Rocks are on beaches.

Rocks are under water.

Rocks are in fields.

Rocks are near homes.

Can Rocks Change?

Rocks are changed by wind.

Rocks are changed by water.

How Do We Use Rocks?

Rocks are used to build.

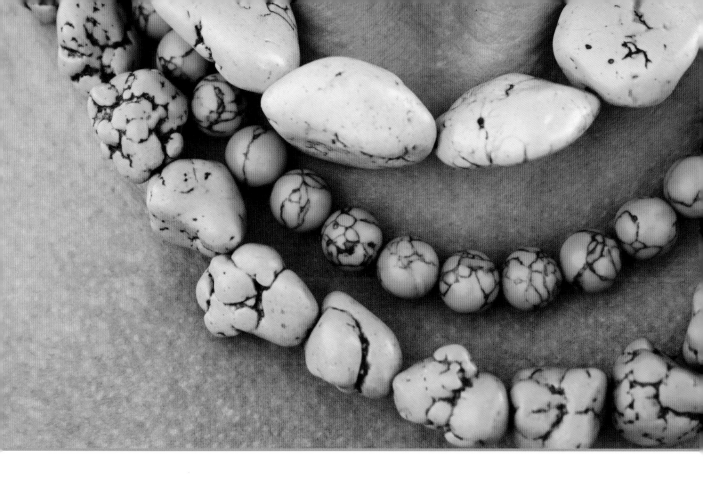

Rocks are used to make jewelry.

Types of Rocks

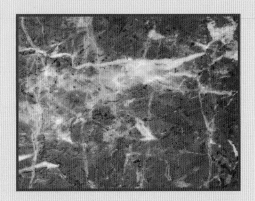

◀ Marble

▲ Diamond

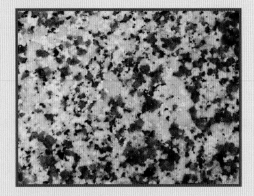

◀ Granite

Picture Glossary

 **beach** area near water. Beaches are covered with sand and rocks.

 **field** open area of land

 **nature** the world around us. Plants, animals, rocks, water, and soil are part of nature.

Content Vocabulary for Teachers

material Something that takes up space and can be used to make other things

natural resource material found in nature that can be used by people

Index

Note to Parents and Teachers

Before reading

Ask children what they know about rocks. Do they see any rocks outside? Do they see any rocks inside? Brainstorm with them about different kinds of rocks. Ask them to guess how rocks are used.

After reading

- Take children outdoors and help them look for rocks. Ask them where they think rocks might be found. Encourage them to look in a variety of locations for rocks.
- Bring a few small rocks back indoors and ask children to sort them into groups of size, color, or texture. Then, ask children to write down descriptive words for each group of rocks.